It Is My Birthday!

by Barbara L. Luciano

Editorial Offices: Glenview, Illinois • Parsippany, New Jersey • New York, New York
Sales Offices: Needham, Massachusetts • Duluth, Georgia • Glenview, Illinois
Coppell, Texas • Sacramento, California • Mesa, Arizona

Birthdays are special!

This child sings.

This child hits a piñata.

4

This child eats pie.

This child rides in a chair.

What do you do?

Glossary

birthday the day you were born

piñata a container filled with
candy, fruit, and small toys
which is hung from the ceiling to
be broken open with bats